BRECON BEACONS

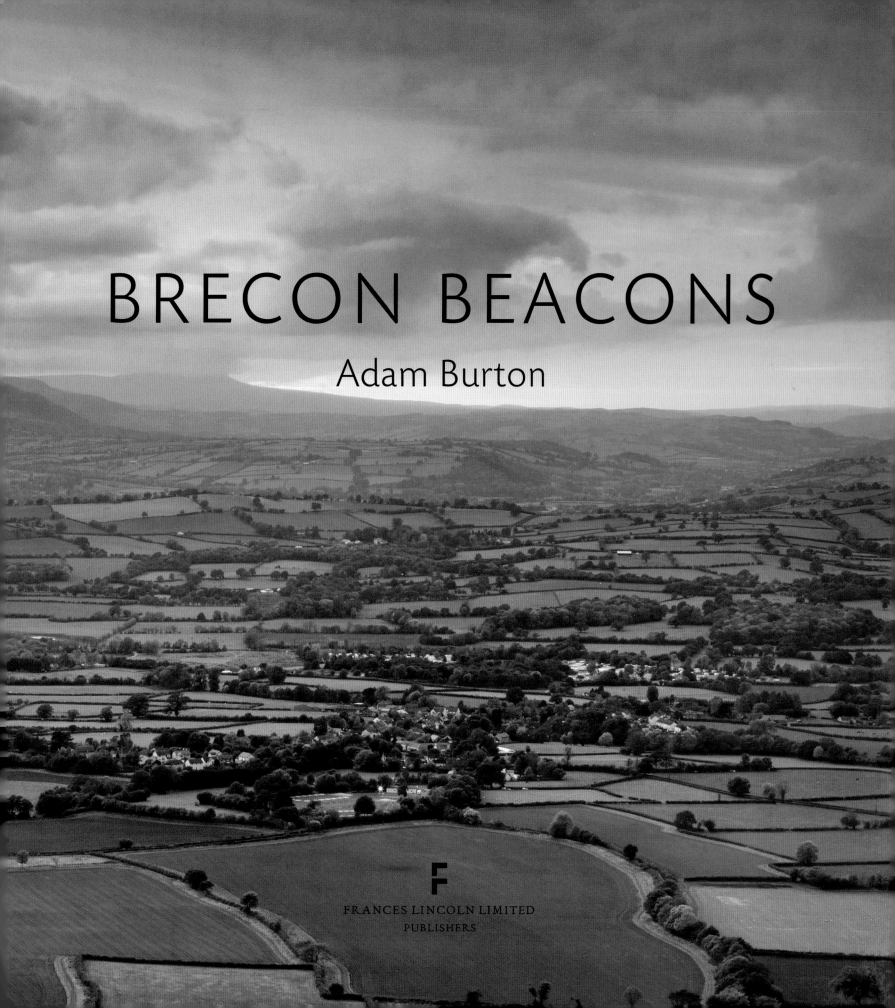

BRECON BEACONS

Adam Burton

F

FRANCES LINCOLN LIMITED
PUBLISHERS

Frances Lincoln Ltd
4 Torriano Mews
Torriano Avenue
London NW5 2RZ
www.franceslincoln.com

Brecon Beacons
Copyright © Frances Lincoln Limited 2011
Text and photographs copyright © Adam Burton 2011
First Frances Lincoln edition 2011

A catalogue record for this book is available
from the British Library.

ISBN: 978-0-7112-3147-4

Printed and bound in China

9 8 7 6 5 4 3 2 1

PAGE 1 Creeping mist approaches the moorland slopes above
Llangynidr. Far above, cloud formations streak spectacular lines
across the morning sky.

PAGE 2–3 Llangorse Lake provides an instantly recognisable
landmark among an ocean of rolling fields. The lake which was
formed in the last ice age from melting glaciers was once around
45 metres higher and would have covered most of the fields
pictured here.

ABOVE Viewed from the northern slopes of Allt yr Esgair,
the summit of Mynydd Troed is a recognisable feature rising
above a sea of mist. Somewhere below the inversion lies
Llangorse Lake, its shores completely immersed with mist
and hidden away from the dawning of this beautiful day.

For little Tom

CONTENTS

An Introduction to the Brecon Beacons 6
Map of the Brecon Beacons 9

Winter 12

Spring 30

Summer 60

Autumn 86

Index and Acknowledgments 112

AN INTRODUCTION TO THE BRECON BEACONS

Established in 1957, the Brecon Beacons was the tenth area of the UK to achieve National Park status, and the last of the three Welsh parks. But don't let this latecomers badge detract from what the park has to offer. Any visitor to the area will immediately understand why the Brecon Beacons is one of Britain's most spectacular and accessible National Parks.

Covering an area of nearly 520 square miles, the Brecon Beacons are dominated by large areas of moorland rising to high mountain summits. In the valleys far below, a sweeping expanse of patchwork fields undulate over gentle rolling hills to make an irresistible and typically British scene. Winding rivers and picturesque canalways pass through this landscape, meandering through pretty rural villages. In wooded valleys, footpaths follow rocky streams that continually tumble over many spectacular waterfalls as they head south to meet the ocean.

The Beacons themselves refer to the ancient practice of lighting signal fires on the mountain tops to warn of invasion. This tradition has continued to the present day, although now only for commemorative purposes such as coronations or the Millennium. Evidence of ancient human habitation is available all over the National Park in the form of Neolithic Standing Stones and Stone Circles, as well as Iron Age hill forts and a Crannog on Llangorse Lake. Throughout history, people have lived and worked in the area, helping to shape many of the landscapes that are now synonymous with the Brecon Beacons.

Our National Parks are referred to as 'Britain's Breathing Spaces'; with so much beautiful and diverse landscape in which to relax and explore, the Brecon Beacons more than deserves its place among this prestigious group.

Mountains and Moorland

There are four mountain ranges within the National Park, all of which are slightly confusing in name. The most famous, and most visited of all the mountains shares the same name as the National Park; the Brecon Beacons. These mountains include Pen y Fan, which at 886metres is the highest peak in Southern Britain. To the east, lying along the border with England are the Black Mountains, which include a stretch of the long distance walking path Offa's Dyke. Further to the west of the Brecon Beacons, the Fforest Fawr is an upland landscape of peaks, moorland and waterfalls, the same name also being used to cover the area's Geopark status. To complete the collection, on the less visited far western edge of the park lies the Black Mountain, not to be confused with the Black Mountains to the east.

Many of the mountains consist of Old Red Sandstone and share distinctive similarities; namely iconic flat summits and deep red mountainside scars. While sometimes requiring steep ascents, the mountains and escarpments of the National Park are generally safe and accessible, making wonderful walking country. The sandstone plateaus provide breathtaking vantage points to rest on fine summer afternoons and gaze down on the landscape below.

But while these mountains are generally welcoming they should not be taken for granted, especially in the unpredictable winter months. Snow, ice, strong winds and extreme temperatures are all frequent visitors to the mountains in winter, and care should be taken when venturing out on such days. It is of no coincidence that the British Army, based in Sennybridge, regularly train in the wilderness areas of the Brecon Beacons. The SAS conduct gruelling selection exercises for potential recruits all over the Brecon Beacons, including the notorious Fan Dance endurance treks over and around Pen y Fan.

Rivers and Waterfalls

While many rivers and streams flow down from the mountains and moorland areas, the great river is the Usk, meandering more than forty miles through the National Park. From its source high up in the Black Mountain beneath Fan Brycheiniog, the River Usk at first descends the uplands in a northwards direction, passing through lonely moorland before reaching the Usk Reservoir. Soon after, it turns eastwards and follows the border of the National Park, meandering through Sennybridge and on to Brecon. At this point, the river turns again, this time heading southeast through the pastoral Usk Valley, passing through many picturesque settlements such as Pencelli and Crickhowell before finally exiting the park near Abergavenny. This majestic river is responsible for the many misty mornings that are synonymous with the Brecon Beacons.

Running along a similar south easterly course as the latter stages of the River Usk, the Monmouthshire and Brecon Canal offers a more tranquil and relaxed alternative to the great rocky river. First opened in the late eighteenth century, the Monmouthshire and Brecon Canal was originally used as a transit mechanism for the coal and iron industries. In recent years the canal has enjoyed a far more peaceful existence, guiding narrowboat holidaymakers along its beautiful rural course.

Due to the process of water erosion of soft Old Red Sandstone layers, several areas of the National Park are famous for waterfalls. Out of all these areas the most spectacular and numerous falls are those found between Ystradfellte and Pontneddfechan, earning this area the title of Waterfall Country. Several rivers, including the Nedd Fechan and Afon Mellte, cascade over a series of stunning drops, each more breathtaking than the last. If you are fortunate you may spot salmon attempting to leap up the waterfalls on their journey upstream.

Reservoirs and Lakes

There is an abundance of picturesque reservoirs and lakes within the mountainous areas of the National Park, including the beautiful sister lakes Llyn y Fan Fach and Llyn y Fan Fawr isolated in the west on the Black Mountain. These lakes lay hidden in the shadow of the mighty Carmarthen Fans, and offer a special feeling of remoteness to those making the effort to hike to them. Llyn y Fan Fach is legendary in Welsh folklore, home to the Lady of the Lake, whose story inspires all who visit.

On the opposite side of the National Park, near the Black Mountains, Llangorse Lake is the largest natural lake in South Wales, and provides an ideal destination for many water based recreational activities. The picturesque lake is often completely shrouded by a heavy blanket of mist at dawn, which gradually evaporates in the morning sunshine to reveal a beautiful backdrop vista of mountains, including the distinctive peak of Pen y Fan. Llangorse Lake is an easily identifiable natural landmark visible from many mountains in both the Brecon Beacons and the Black Mountains.

Hills and Countryside

Away from the wild moors and mountains, the countryside of the Brecon Beacons is picture postcard material. Picturesque green hedgerows separate endless stretches of rolling patchwork fields, dotted with the occasional mature tree, tractors and cattle. In the winter season fields are a swathe of lush green, while summer brings about a striking change as ripening crops colour fields in golden tones, and bales are dotted all over the landscape.

For those seeking the tranquillity of such pastoral countryside, the fertile Usk Valley near Crickhowell is an area not to be missed. Many footpaths criss-cross the rolling countryside near here, or for the more energetic, walks onto the hills around the Llangattock Escarpment will provide splendid vistas over the green and pleasant land.

A Photographer's Journey

The photographs contained within this book are the result of a year wandering the Brecon Beacons. They are a hand picked selection of favourite images, and together intended as a collective personal vision of the Brecon Beacons landscapes rather than an exhaustive guide to the area. For me, this was an almost entirely new location and somewhat of a challenge for a photographer based in Devon. But the experience of exploring and capturing the natural landscapes of the area is something I will forever cherish. From my very first trip back in the summer of 2009 I was absolutely captivated by the scenery and immediately became addicted to exploring and photographing more of the National Park.

I was extremely fortunate with the weather. Aside from the occasional abandoned trip due to severe rain, I was mostly lucky to encounter beautiful and sometimes magical weather conditions. I have lost count of the number of mornings I have woken to encounter blankets of mist hanging over the landscape. The only challenge was to ascend hilltops and position myself above the mist, sometimes starting my ascent at 3am in complete darkness. But even on the moments when conditions were not suitable for photography, the vantage point more than warranted the journey.

The most challenging season was undoubtedly winter, when the coldest snap for many years left the Beacons coated in layers of snow and ice. During this period access to many locations within the park proved impossible, and the few roads that were passable were still slippery and dangerous. On a particularly wintry morning I remember walking over the moorland to Llyn y Fan Fawr in the Black Mountains. After trudging through deep snow I eventually reached the lake, frozen over and surrounded by mysterious hill fog; it felt like I had walked into a lonely alien landscape. After a couple of wrong steps I soon found myself up to my waist in snow, but somehow managed to pull myself out before continuing on my journey, albeit more cautiously.

Throughout a year of extensively photographing the Brecon Beacons for this book, my enthusiasm and passion for this area has continually grown. I hope that, through the photographs contained on the following pages, I can share some of my passion for this beautiful location and inspire you to keep returning to this special place for many years to come.

Beautiful rolling countryside surrounding Bwlch awakens with the arrival of spring. On the far horizon, the familiar landmark of the Sugar Loaf peaks above the valley slopes.

PAGE 7: A tree which had for a long time leaned precariously over Horseshoe Falls had finally fallen on my last autumn trip to the Nedd Fechan. It was now firmly trapped between both banks, to no doubt remain there until flood waters or decay dislodge and carry it further down the river.

MAP OF THE BRECON BEACONS

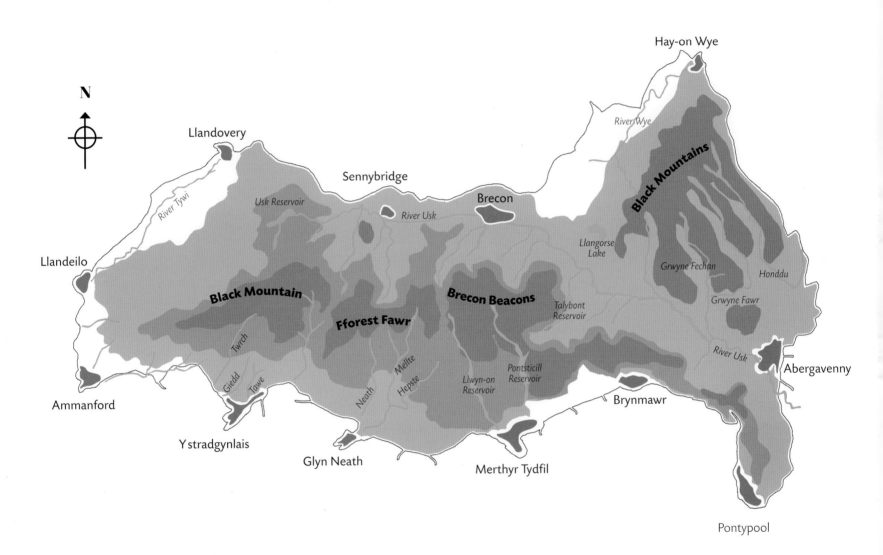

N

Hay-on Wye

Llandovery

Sennybridge

Brecon

River Wye

River Tywi

Usk Reservoir

River Usk

Black Mountains

Llandeilo

Llangorse Lake

Black Mountain

Grwyne Fechan

Honddu

Brecon Beacons

Grwyne Fawr

Fforest Fawr

Talybont Reservoir

Twrch

River Usk

Gledd

Mellte

Tawe

Hepste

Pontsticill Reservoir

Abergavenny

Llwyn-on Reservoir

Neath

Ammanford

Brynmawr

Ystradgynlais

Glyn Neath

Merthyr Tydfil

Pontypool

winter

Perfect reflections in the still waters of the Upper Neuadd Reservoir on a cold January afternoon.

Bracken is cut each autumn by the National Park Authority, to be used as an alternative to straw as bedding for livestock. Bracken is not only cheaper than straw bedding, but hardier and more absorbant. The bales can also be stored outside with little degradation.

RIGHT: Snow covered circular bracken bales scattered over Mynydd Illtud Common in wintertime.

Fading sunlight softly illuminates the snow covered peaks of Corn Du and Pen y Fan on a January evening.

A frozen and snow covered pond on Mynydd Illtud Common, looking towards the Brecon Beacons mountain range.

Frozen scenes at Llangorse Lake on a bitterly cold January morning.

Lying at the foot of Fan Brycheiniog, Llyn y Fan Fawr is a remote lake in the Black Mountain range of the National Park. Pictured here on a foggy and freezing winter morning, the lake, which lies at 605 metres above sea level, is partially frozen over.

Looking southwest to the snow covered peak of Fan Fawr from the Beacons Way footpath on the slopes of Corn Du.

From an elevation of 800 metres the moorland, mountains and rolling countryside of the Brecon Beacons National Park merges into one continuous white blanket during winter snowfall.

Finger sized tubes of ice coat each blade of grass brave enough to protrude through the thick blanket of snow on the mountainside below Corn Du.

A light dusting of snow remains on the hillside slope of Allt yr Esgair at the end of a cold clear winter day.

Various footpaths provide routes up the ridge of Allt yr Esgair. The summit provides wonderful views in all directions.

Completed in 1955, the Usk Reservoir is situated among forest and moorland in one of the least visited areas of the National Park. These boats, safely pulled up out of the water are used for fishing; the reservoir is highly regarded as one of the best trout fisheries in Wales.

The Bronze Age standing stone Maen Mawr is located on open moorland, near the source of the River Tawe. Like the many other standing stones in Wales, Maen Mawr was protected by an ancient Welsh law which carried the death penalty for anybody found to be harming it. Due to this law, many standing stones have been preserved and still exist to this day in the National Park.

Just a few metres away from Maen Mawr standing stone is another ancient monument, the Cerrig Duon stone circle. Although classed as a stone circle, the stones are actually positioned in an egg shape, which is exceptionally rare in Britain. Pictured here behind a frozen pool are two of the stones which make up the circle.

The River Tawe near its source is nothing more than
a gurgling stream, tumbling over a series of rocks as it
journeys south towards Swansea.

Pink tinted clouds above Graig Fan Ddu add a splash of warm colour to the icy Upper Neuadd Reservoir at sunset.

As clouds of hill fog swirl over the snow covered mountain side, Llyn y Fan Fawr is temporarily revealed in its magnificent entirety. But within moments of taking this image, the lake would once again disappear in the mysterious creeping fog.

Dry stone walls on the moorland slopes of Moel Feity look like the abandoned ruins of an old farmhouse. Whatever their original purpose could have been, they now provide shelter from the elements for free roaming sheep.

Melting snow on the shores of the Upper Neuadd Reservoir, looking north towards Cribyn.

spring

The picturesque undulating mini-hills of the
Llangattock Escarpment are not natural features of
the landscape. They are the remnants from a period of
extensive quarrying of the limestone landscape starting in
the late eighteenth century, originally for the construction
of the Monmouthshire and Brecon Canal. Since quarrying
stopped over 60 years ago, the area has been reclaimed by
nature and now offers a unique and beautiful location
to explore.

Looking down from the mountain summit Picws Du over
Llyn y Fan Fach. At 749 metres Picws Du is the highest point in
the Carmarthen Fans. This ridge in the Black Mountain is every bit
as spectacular as Pen y Fan to the east and yet is far less visited.

RIGHT: A lonely isolated lake situated high in the Black Mountain,
Llyn y Fan Fach is steeped in Welsh folklore. According to legend
this is the home of the fabled Lady of the Lake whose story also
connects the location with the Physicians of Myddfai.

These trees on the slopes of Mynydd Llanwenarth look as though
they are out of sync with the seasons; their golden leaves seem ready
to drop for the winter months. In truth they are covered with new
spring foliage, the leaves backlit by the low sunshine.

LEFT: A lone hawthorn tree bathes in late evening sunlight on
the slopes of the Sugar Loaf near Abergavenny.

Limestone rock debris scatters the
moorland slopes above the Llangattock
Escarpment. Starting on the left of the
frame, the peaks on the horizon are the
Sugar Loaf, Ysgyryd Fawr and Ysgyryd Fach.

Just before the morning sun makes its first appearance, a fiery ray of light bursts upwards into the cloudy sky above the Sugar Loaf.

A ramshackle yet characterful dry stone wall separates farmland from the moorland slopes of Mynydd Llanwenarth. Hopefully, the replacement wire fence is only a temporary solution until the magnificent wall, which has no doubt stood for many generations, can be restored.

A young sapling in vibrant spring foliage clings to the cliffside edge
of Llangattock Escarpment. On the horizon, sunrise emerges
directly behind the iconic Sugar Loaf mountain.

Far reaching views can be enjoyed from the Llangattock Escarpment. Pictured here, the mountains of Mynydd Llangorse and Mynydd Troed are clearly visible despite being around ten miles away.

In late April and early May the woods of Coed Cefn near
Crickhowell spring vividly to life with carpets of Common
Bluebells matched above by a canopy of vibrant new foliage.

Preserved by the Woodland Trust, Coed Cefn Wood lies on the site of an Iron Age hill fort. Most of the woodland comprises Oak and Beech trees, as pictured here.

Beautiful pastoral countryside is revealed through
patches of swirling mist at dawn on a tranquil
spring morning near Pennorth.

Cefn Moel rises above the cloud inversion, viewed from Allt yr Esgair.

RIGHT: Viewed from the northern slopes of Allt yr Esgair, the summit of Mynydd Troed is a recognisable feature rising above a sea of mist. Somewhere below the inversion lies Llangorse Lake, its shores completely immersed with mist and hidden away from the dawning of this beautiful day.

A series of waterfalls cascade over sandstone ledges all along this stretch of the River Ennig at Pwll-y-Wrach Nature Reserve.

LEFT: The Pwll-y-Wrach Nature Reserve near Talgarth is a steep valley formed from erosion of the Old Red Sandstone layers by the River Ennig. The rocks here are around 400 million years old and reveal clues to environmental change that took place at this time.

Throughout a year of photographing
the Brecon Beacons I've been fortunate to
witness many cloud inversions. Viewed here
from the summit of Allt yr Esgair, the blanket
of cloud clings against the lower slopes of
the Usk Valley. On the distant horizon the
silhouette of Pen y Fan is visible against
a pastel pink dawn sky.

Mist blankets the hills and mountains surrounding
the Usk Valley at dawn.

RIGHT: Bluebells, ferns and wild garlic carpet the banks
either side of the River Ennig during springtime.

Bluebells growing alongside a pretty rural footpath running between tree lined fields.

RIGHT: A tranquil early morning vista from the mist shrouded shores of Llangorse Lake.

The thatched building is a modern reconstruction of an Iron Age Crannóg. Close to this reconstruction, an authentic Crannóg (or man-made island dwelling) has been excavated. According to historical evidence the Crannóg was a royal residence known as Brycheiniog.

RIGHT: A sunny spring afternoon beside the picturesque Monmouthshire and Brecon Canal near Pencelli.

New spring foliage hangs in a verdant canopy over
the peaceful canal waters near Llanhamlach.

The original purpose of this towpath would have been for horses to walk along, towing barges up and down the canal. Nowadays it provides a relaxing level footpath for walkers, cyclists and runners.

A carpet of bluebells in unfamiliar territory adorns the open western slopes of Ysgyryd Fawr (also known as The Skirrid). The lush rolling countryside beyond has seen the last of the sunshine on this day, as it sinks behind hazy clouds above the Sugar Loaf.

From The Skirrid the town of Abergavenny, lying just outside the National Park border, is just visible.

From the top of Ysgyryd Fawr sweeping views can be enjoyed east over Herefordshire and west back over the countryside and Black Mountains of the National Park. Ysgyryd Fawr was a favourite walking route of Rudolf Hess, while he was a prisoner in nearby Maindiff Court during World War Two.

summer

Rich summer evening light bathes the southern shores of Llangorse Lake and the steep slopes of Mynydd Troed in the Black Mountains.

Late evening sunlight illuminates the patchwork of
farmland on the slopes of the Usk Valley. In the far
distance the mountains of Cribyn and Pen y Fan slowly
become enveloped by low cloud.

This dry stone wall runs along the ridge of Allt yr Esgair (commonly
referred to as 'The Allt'). An Iron Age fort once stood at the summit,
its inhabitants no doubt recognising the benefits of The Allt's natural
defences and far reaching views.

When conditions are right, the deep valleys of the Brecon Beacons can often experience early morning mist. Pictured here, lingering mist blankets the countryside beneath the Black Mountains at dawn.

Creeping mist approaches the moorland slopes above Llangynidr. Far above, cloud formations streak spectacular lines across the morning sky.

Although barely a trickle in summer, at nearly 30 metres Henrhyd Falls
is the tallest waterfall in South Wales. A fallen tree, probably carried down
the Nant Llech and over the waterfall, now lies stranded in the shallow
waters at the base of the gorge.

RIGHT: The Nedd Fechan presents a beautiful sight as it cascades over the
Scwd Ddwli waterfall, hidden in the wooded gorge near Pont Melin-fach.
Together with its neighbouring river the Afon Mellte, this area is famous
for its many spectacular waterfalls.

Picws Du and Fan Foel are two of the highest peaks that make up the Carmarthen Fans in the Black Mountain area of the National Park. The mountains' sandstone origins are evident in the deep red scars on the steep slopes, accentuated by the warm tones of the late evening sunlight.

Equally as spectacular as its wild mountain areas, the rolling countryside of the Brecon Beacons is a remarkable sight to behold. Luckily the hills and mountains provide an almost infinite number of lofty viewpoints from which to gaze at the beautiful landscape below.

Wild foxgloves add a splash of vibrant colour to the bracken covered slopes below Cefn Moel.

The Black Mountains peak of Pen Allt-Mawr emerges above
a mist shrouded valley near the village of Cwmdu. Mist has
the ability to transform mornings such as this into scenes
almost otherworldly in appearance.

Mist diffuses the rays of early morning sunlight beside this
moorland road from Llangynidr to Beaufort.

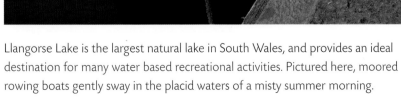

Llangorse Lake is the largest natural lake in South Wales, and provides an ideal destination for many water based recreational activities. Pictured here, moored rowing boats gently sway in the placid waters of a misty summer morning.

A burst of sunshine radiates from the Sugar Loaf
at dawn, illuminating the slopes beneath the
limestone escarpment at Craig y Cilau.

As the River Caerfanell descends from high moorland to deep wooded valleys, it drops through a series of waterfalls at Blaen-y-Glyn. While these may be some of the lesser known waterfalls of the National Park, their scenic location makes them an idyllic destination to explore.

Vibrant green ferns cluster on the banks of the rocky stream Caerfanell.

The majority of woodland within the National Park consists of coniferous plantations, but this wasn't always the case. As with most other areas of the UK, many thousands of years ago the lowland landscapes were covered with deciduous woodland. Here, a magnificent deciduous tree stands proud in a conifer plantation.

Moss covered remains of an old dry stone wall in a pine plantation at Blaen-y-Glyn.

With medieval origins, St. Illtyd's church in the village of Llanhamlach has long stood in the shadow of the Brecon Beacon mountains.

First opened in the late eighteenth century, the Monmouthshire and Brecon Canal was originally used as a transit mechanism for the coal and iron industries. In recent years the canal has enjoyed a far more peaceful existence, guiding narrowboat holidaymakers along its beautiful rural course.

Peaceful rolling farmland bathed in soft evening light, looking north towards the Black Mountains.

A tranquil early morning scene showing
the village of Capel Gwynfe surrounded by
an endless patchwork of green fields.

Viewed from the slopes of Foel Nant Dwyn at dawn, the rolling
pastoral landscape awakens in a dreamlike swirl of early morning mist.

TOP RIGHT: Early morning mist clings to the countryside near
Twynllanan in the less visited western side of the National Park.

BOTTOM RIGHT: On the remote western side of the Brecon
Beacons National Park, the spectacular Carreg Cennen Castle
dominates the surrounding landscape. Perched high on a limestone
precipice the castle, which was built in the twelfth century, is visible
for many miles around.

Despite being an impressive 795 metres in height, the sandstone
mountain Cribyn (on the right of the picture) can be looked
down upon from the summit of Pen y Fan. The mountains of
the Brecon Beacons are the highest in southern Britain and offer
unbroken vistas for a great many miles.

autumn

The Taf Fechan river has its source on the slopes of Pen y Fan in the Brecon Beacons mountain range. It runs southwards to Merthyr Tydfil where it merges with the Taf Fawr to form the River Taf, eventually reaching the sea at Cardiff. Pictured here, the river is still a rocky stream as it tumbles through the Taf Fechan Forest.

A vista that captures what is so special about the Brecon Beacons National Park. An exceptionally beautiful sweeping expanse of gently sunlit fields and tree lined hedgerows, dotted with pockets of quickly evaporating morning mist. Rising above the distant fields the Black Mountains overlook the breathtaking rolling landscape.

A mist covered autumnal landscape at dawn
on the outskirts of Bwlch.

The Lower Neuadd Reservoir marks the start of the famous Beacons Horseshoe Trail. The six mile circular route passes the summits of Cribyn, Pen y Fan and Corn Du before returning to the reservoir via the Graig Fan Ddu escarpment (pictured).

Late afternoon sunlight illuminates the beautiful
countryside near the village of Llangorse.

The River Ennig cascades over rocks in a series of waterfalls
at Pwll-y-Wrach Nature Reserve near Talgarth.

TOP RIGHT: Sheep graze on the steep sided slopes of the Vale of
Ewyas, above which the Hatterall Ridge forms a natural boundary
between England and Wales. Along the summit of the ridge runs
the Offa's Dyke long distance footpath.

BOTTOM RIGHT: The picturesque ruins of twelfth century Llanthony
Priory lie in the secluded Vale of Ewyas within the Black Mountains.

A golden pre-dawn glow colours the sky above the dark and misty Usk Valley. On the horizon the distinctive outline of the Sugar Loaf marks the eastern fringes of the National Park.

High moorland footpath over the summit of Tor y Foel, looking south into the Glyn Collwn Valley.

Early morning sun bathes Abercynafon and the Glyn Collwn Valley in beautiful golden light. Just visible at the head of the valley are the tranquil waters of the Talybont Reservoir.

Looking south to Corn Du and Pen y Fan mountains
from Mynydd Illtud in the last light of day.

One of the many stone bridges along the Monmouthshire and Brecon Canal, reflected perfectly in the still waters of an October morning.

Although only 37 miles in length, the Monmouthshire and Brecon Canal is one of the most beautiful waterways in the UK. Most of the canal is situated within the National Park, where narrowboat holidaymakers can enjoy peace and tranquillity while cruising through wonderful surroundings.

A mysterious and ethereal Llangorse Lake is revealed beneath the lingering mist in the pre-dawn light from the slopes of Mynydd Llangorse.

The Afon Mellte tumbles through a series of cascades near the village of Ystradfellte. Due to the plethera of cascades along both this river and its neighbours the Nedd Fechan, Afon Pyrddin and Afon Hepste, this area has become known as 'Waterfall Country'.

The best time to visit the wooded gorge of the Afon Mellte is late autumn, when the varied range of deciduous trees put on a rich display of colour. Pictured here, Sgwd Clun-Gwyn waterfall cascades some 10 metres over a stepped sandstone drop.

Lying at the base of a deep gorge Sgwd yr Eira carries the Afon Hepste crashing down a vertical drop. This is perhaps the most famous of all the Brecon Beacons' many waterfalls, and even has a path allowing walkers to pass behind the falls.

With its wide cascade and secluded setting Scwd Ddwli is one of the prettiest waterfalls in the Brecon Beacons. As I photographed a little further downstream I noticed the occasional salmon relentlessly attempting to leap up cascades. Their incredible determination to head upstream must surely be in vain when faced with impossible barriers such as Scwd Ddwli.

TOP LEFT: Farm buildings in the countryside near Bwlch.

BOTTOM LEFT: The tree lined hedgerows near Bwlch slowly turn golden as autumn progresses towards winter.

A network of footpaths between Pontneddfechan and Ystradfellte provide convenient access to each of the rivers in 'Waterfall Country', making this a popular spot for walking.

LEFT: The Afon Pyrddin cascades over a natural sandstone ledge at Sgwd Gwladus. Sgwd Gwladus translates as The Lady's Falls; the lady in question was a daughter of Brychan, the fifth century King of Brycheinog.

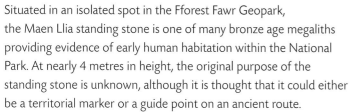

Situated in an isolated spot in the Fforest Fawr Geopark, the Maen Llia standing stone is one of many bronze age megaliths providing evidence of early human habitation within the National Park. At nearly 4 metres in height, the original purpose of the standing stone is unknown, although it is thought that it could either be a territorial marker or a guide point on an ancient route.

An isolated farm on the slopes of the Senni Valley.

The River Caerfanell plunges over a vertical drop at Blaen-y-Glyn
before continuing its course towards the Talybont Reservoir.

Rich autumnal colours surround the Caerfanell valley near Blaen-y-Glyn.

INDEX

A

Abergavenny 6, 33, 57
Afon Mellte 7, 66, 102/3
Afon Pyrddin 102, 107
Allt yr Esgair 4, 20, 42, 47, 62

B

Black Mountain 6/7, 8, 16, 30, 68
Black Mountains 6, 8, 57, 59, 63, 70, 77, 86, 92
Blaen-y-Glyn 74/5, 110/11
Bwlch 8, 88, 105

C

Capel Gwynfe 79
Carmarthen Fans 7, 30, 68
Carreg Cennen 80
Cefn Moel 42, 69
Cerrig Duon 23
Coed Cefn 38/9
Corn Du 14, 18/19, 89, 97
Craig y Cilau 73
Cribyn 27, 60, 82, 89
Crickhowell 6, 8, 38
Cwmdu 70

F

Fan Brycheiniog 6, 16
Fan Foel 68
Fforest Fawr 6, 108
Foel Nant Dwyn 80

G

Glyn Collwn 96
Graig Fan Ddu 26, 89

H

Henrhyd Falls 66

L

Llangattock Escarpment 8, 29, 34, 36/7
Llangorse Lake 4, 6, 8, 15, 42, 50, 52, 59, 72, 101
Llangynidr 4, 65, 71
Llanhamlach 54, 76
Llanthony Priory 92
Llyn y Fan Fach 7, 30
Llyn y Fan Fawr 7, 8, 16, 26

M

Maen Mawr 22/3
Moel Feity 27
Monmouthshire and Brecon Canal 6, 29, 52, 54/5, 76, 98/9
Mynydd Illtud 12, 14, 97
Mynydd Llangorse 37, 101
Mynydd Llanwenarth 33, 35
Mynydd Troed 4, 37, 42, 59

N

Nedd Fechan 7, 66, 102
Neuadd Reservoir 11, 26/7, 89

O

Offa's Dyke 6, 92

P

Pen Allt-Mawr 70
Pen y Fan 6, 8, 14, 30, 47, 60, 82, 85, 89, 97
Pencelli 6, 52
Pennorth 41
Picws Du 30, 68
Pontneddfechan 7, 107
Pwll-y-Wrach 45, 92

R

River Caerfanell 74, 110/11
River Ennig 45, 48, 92
River Tawe 22, 24

S

Scwd Ddwli 66, 105
Senni Valley 109
Sgwd Clun-gwyn 103
Sgwd Gwladus 107
Sgwd yr Eira 103
Skirrid 56/7
Standing Stones 22/3, 108
Sugar Loaf 8, 33, 34/5, 36, 56, 73, 94

T

Taf Fechan 85
Talgarth 45, 92
Talybont Reservoir 96, 110
Tor y Foel 96
Twynllanan 80

U

Usk Reservoir 6, 21
Usk Valley 6, 8, 47, 48, 60, 94

V

Vale of Ewyas 92

W

Waterfall 6/7, 45, 66, 74, 92, 102/3, 105, 107, 110

Y

Ysgyryd Fach 34
Ysgyryd Fawr 34, 56/7
Ystradfellte 7, 102, 107

ACKNOWLEDGMENTS

I would like to thank the following people who have helped me in the making of this book:

Beth Burton
Andrew Dunn
Ian Munro
Phil Morgan
John Nicoll
Mari Owen

Adam Burton's images are distributed by the following agencies or direct from www.adamburtonphotography.com:

- *Photolibrary (www.photolibrary.com)*
- *Alamy (www.alamy.com)*
- *Britain on View (www.britainonview.com)*
- *Robert Harding Picture Library (www.robertharding.com)*
- *Nature Picture Library (www.naturepl)*

For prints, commissions, photo sales, workshops and any other enquiries please visit www.adamburtonphotography.com or contact Adam at info@adamburtonphotography.com.